The Songs of TIN PAN ALLEY for Ukulele

ARRANGED BY

DICK SHERIDAN

Design & Typography by **Roy "Rick" Dains**
FalconMarketingMedia@gmail.com
Cover Ukulele Photo by **Ron Middlebrook**
Koa Ukulele with Rope Binding Courtesy of **National Reso-Phonic**

To access audio, visit:
www.HalLeonard.com/MyLibrary
Enter Code
1294-4151-3953-4246

ISBN 978-1-57424-327-7

Copyright ©2016 CENTERSTREAM Publishing, LLC
P. O. Box 17878 - Anaheim Hills, CA 92817
email: centerstream@aol.com • **web:** centerstream-usa.com

Song Listing

About the Author

Figuratively speaking, Dick Sheridan was brought up in the shadow of Tin Pan Alley. His dad was a good amateur piano player whose generation coincided with the heyday of music publishing on 28th Street in New York City. Whether from sheet music or by ear, Dick's dad played all the popular tunes of the day. It was the exposure to this music and Dick's love of it that inspired him to learn to play these songs himself. It started by first vamping chords on the piano and playing duets with his dad, then by scouring tune and method books so he could learn to play the uke and make the songs his own.

Because of his uke playing, Dick was recruited in college to join a campus Dixieland jazz band and exchange the ukulele for a banjo. He discovered that many of the Tin Pan Alley songs he grew up with were the basis of the group's repertoire, and this continues to be so with the band Dick currently leads that has been in existence for almost 50 years.

But the ukulele was never far from reach either in college jam sessions or the intervening years that followed. Even today, now a century after they were first written, the songs from Tin Pan Alley continue to top Dick's list of favorites. It's no wonder since they remain just as fresh as when they were first penned, full of the vitality that makes them perpetually popular and loads of fun to play.

Dick is eager to share the enjoyment he has found playing the songs and tunes included in this book. They form a terrific collection, one that is truly representative of the wonderful world of yesterday and the best from the Golden Age of music flowing from that unique and enduring institution called Tin Pan Alley.

Introduction

Think back to the late 1800s and the start of the Twentieth Century. Picture horse-drawn carriages, delivery drays and trolleys. Recall gaslight street lamps, bowler hats and derbies, high-button shoes, skirts that reached to the ankle, and flamboyant millinery creations as wide as outstretched elbows. But more, think of a street in the Union Square district of New York City and a row of four-story buildings emanating from which was a cacophony of pounding pianos and singing voices, all performing simultaneously, all sending out a head-spinning mix of completely different songs and music. Think Tin Pan Alley!

The location was 28th Street in Manhattan, situated between Fifth Avenue and Broadway.

It was the center of sheet music publishing with side-by-side offices and studios of numerous publishers on every building's floor. A journalist described the street as a racket of noise that resembled the sound of banging tin pans. He called it "Tin Pan Alley" – and the name stuck.

Although sound recordings were just emerging, sheet music was the way songs were popularized, and it was big business. Some songs sold tens of thousands of copies bringing enormous profits to publishers and huge rewards to song writers.

Understandably there was great competition among publishing firms, each trying to outdo their competitors and capture a share of the market for themselves. Every effort was made

Introduction

Famous Tin Pan Alley composers include such greats as (left to right): George Gershwin, Irving Berlin and Cole Porter.

by publishers to bring their songs to the public. Song pluggers toured the city's cabarets and theater districts with their firm's latest output. Show business folk and vaudeville entertainers were lured into the studios to hear the current offerings, the hope of publishers being that their songs would be performed by noted celebrities who would then inspire the public to rush out and buy copies of the music.

The heyday of Tin Pan Alley spanned over 30 years. It was a time of immensely creative and prolific song writers, many of whom had started off as song pluggers. The names of George Gershwin, Gus Edwards, Gus Kahn, Walter Donaldson and Albert Von Tilzer were legendary. Some like Irving Berlin even started their own publishing companies.

Entertainers from the world of show business relied on Tin Pan Alley as a source for their music, and many gained prominence from the songs they sang. But not all songs were successful and it was hard to predict what would capture the public's fancy and become the next mega hit. There were plenty of duds but also great successes, and the songs in this book show how popular and enduring some have continued to be.

It is remarkable in a sense that so many songs that emerged from Tin Pan Alley – now over 100 hundred years ago – have held their place in the market. But then, if you consider how classical music has lasted for hundreds of years it portends a great future for Tin Pan Alley.

The sheet music boom was not just for piano players. The ukulele rose to ascendancy during this time and it fully shared the output of Tin Pan Alley. No doubt about it, the uke was responsible for putting much of the roar into the Roaring Twenties as well as contributing no small amount to the decades that followed

Over the years ukulele players have kept the momentum going and now the baton is passed to you. The legacy of Tin Pan Alley is truly rich and rewarding. It encompasses treasures that never seem to grow old, that are continually being rediscovered -- a timeless, wonderful world of regenerating vintage song that clearly shows what's old is new again.

Alabama Jubilee

Ukulele tuning: gCEA

JACK YELLEN

GEORGE L .COBB

Alabama Jubilee

Alice Blue Gown

Ukulele tuning: gCEA

JOSEPH McCARTHY

HARRY TIERNEY

Alice Blue Gown

All By Myself

Ukulele tuning: gCEA

IRVING BERLIN

All By Myself

April Showers

Ukulele tuning: gCEA

B.G. DeSYLVA

LOUIS SILVERS

April Showers

Ballin' the Jack

Ukulele tuning: gCEA

JIM BURRIS

CHRIS SMITH

Ballin' the Jack

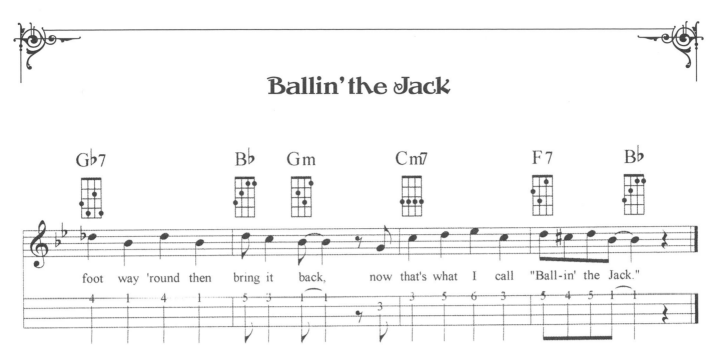

foot way 'round then bring it back, now that's what I call "Ball-in' the Jack."

Note: The "Eagle Rock" was a popular African-American dance where the arms were outstretched and the body rocked from side to side.

Danny Kaye performed his rendition of *"Ballin' The Jack"* in the 20th Century Fox Motion Picture, *"On The Riviera"* (1951).

By the Light of the Silvery Moon

Ukulele tuning: gCEA

EDWARD MADDEN

GUS EDWARDS

By the Light of the Silvery Moon

Note: For ease of playing, try substituting a barre across all strings on the 3rd fret for Eb and Cm chords.

Carolina in the Morning

Ukulele tuning: gCEA

GUS KAHN   WALTER DONALDSON

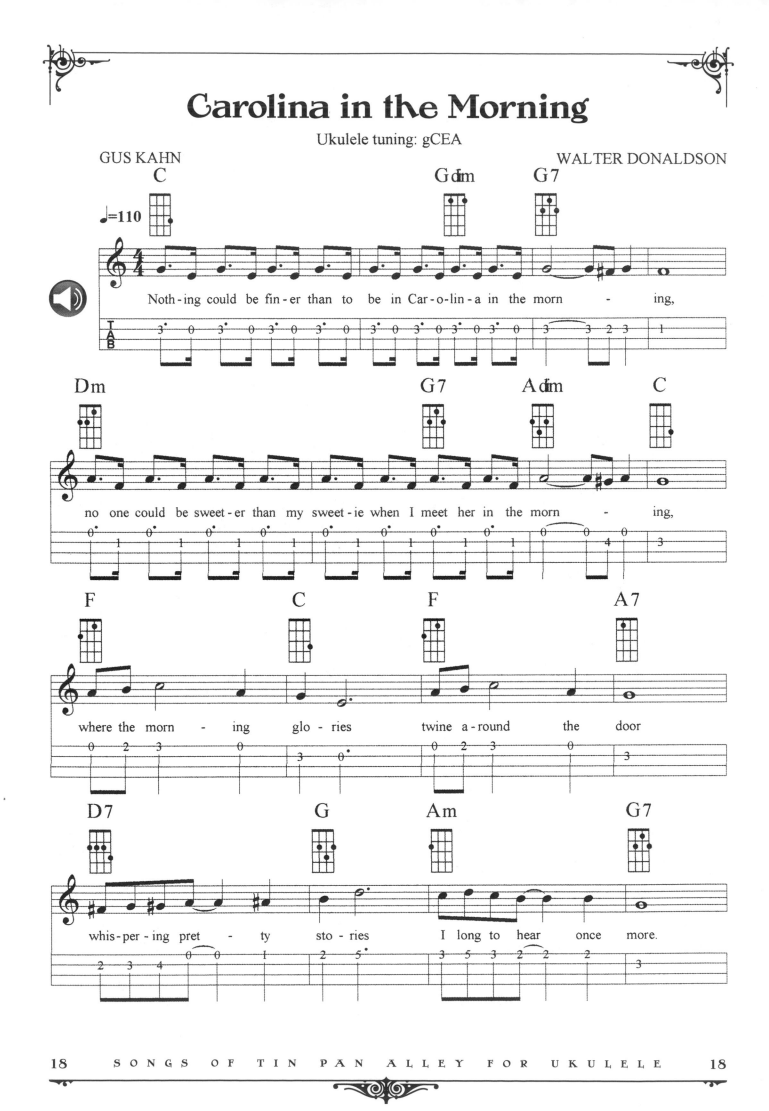

Carolina in the Morning

Chicago

Ukulele tuning: gCEA

FRED FISHER

Chicago

Billy Sunday was a former professional ball player who became an evangelist. He preached against the evils of drink and was a supporter of prohibition.

Max Zides and **Tom Currier**, known as the stage act, **Hum and Strum**, were famous musicians and singers in Vaudeville, Radio and Television. Their extensive repertoire of music included many of the great songs from *Tin Pan Alley*.

Cuddle Up a Little Closer

Ukulele tuning: gCEA

KARL HOSCHNA

Darktown Strutters' Ball

Ukulele tuning: gCEA

SHELTON BROOKS

Darktown Strutters' Ball

D7 **F**

two - steps, I'm goin' to have 'em all,___ goin' to dance out both my

B7 **C** **E7** **A7**

shoes, when they play the "Jel - ly Roll Blues,"___ to -

D7 **G7** **C**

mor - row night___ at the Dark - town Strut - ters' Ball.

Dill Pickles Rag

Ukulele tuning: gCEA

CHARLES L. JOHNSON

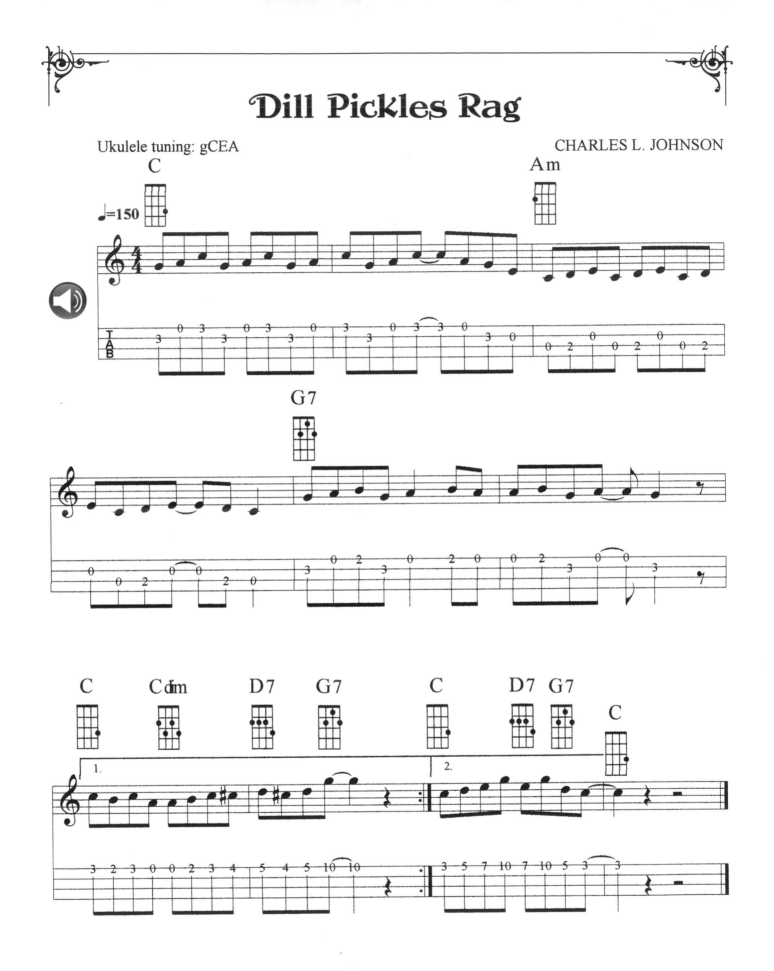

Charles L. Johnson (1876-1950): composer of *"Dill Pickles Rag"* as well as over 300 popular and ragtime songs. His most famous song was a sentimental ballad called, *"Sweet and Low,"* which sold over a million copies.

Down in Jungle Town

Ukulele tuning: gCEA

EDWARD MADDEN   THEODORE MORSE

Down in Jungle Town

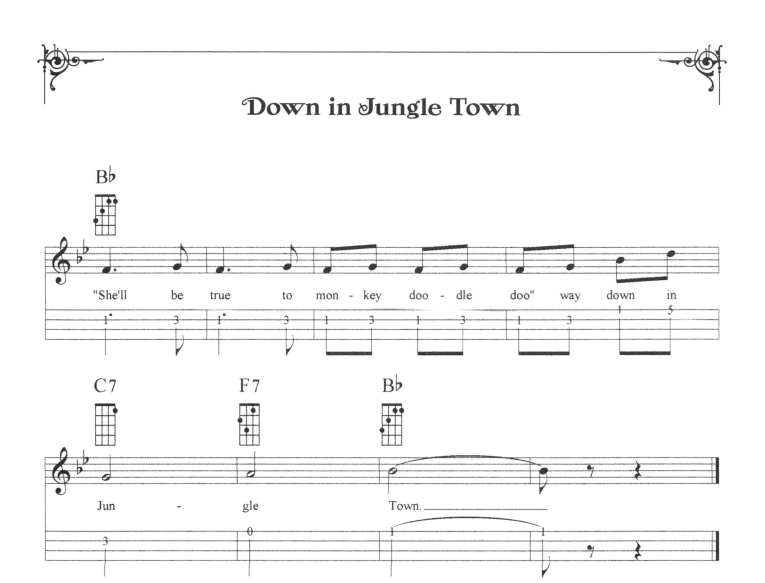

"She'll be true to mon-key doo-dle doo" way down in Jun-gle Town.

A wacky, whimsical version of *"Down in Jungle Town"* was recorded by **Spike Jones and His City Slickers** in 1943, with a vocal by **Del Porter.**

For Me and My Gal

Ukulele tuning: gCEA

GEORGE W. MEYER, EDGAR LESLIE, E. RAY GOETZ

For Me and My Gal

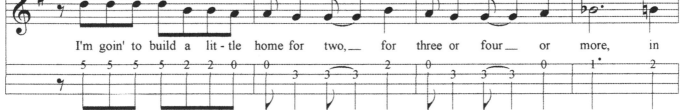

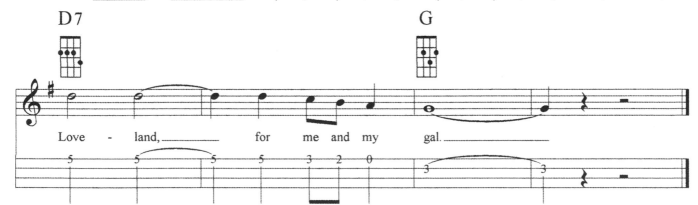

I Want a Girl

Ukulele tuning: gCEA

WILLIAM DILLON

HARRY VON TILZER

I Wonder Who's Kissing Her Now

Ukulele tuning: gCEA

WILL M. HOUGH & FRANK R. ADAMS   JOSEPH E. HOWARD

If I Had My Way

Ukulele tuning: gCEA

LOU KLEIN

JAMES KENDIS

If I Had My Way

If You Were the Only Girl In the World

Ukulele tuning: gCEA

CLIFFORD GREY

NAT D. AYER

If You Were the Only Girl In the World

(continued on next page)

If You Were the Only Girl
In the World

(continued)

you were the on - ly girl in the world and

I was the on - ly boy.

continued

Indiana
(Back Home Again in Indiana)

Ukulele tuning: gCEA

BALLARD MacDONALD

JAMES F. HANLEY

Back home a-gain___ in In-di-an-a and it seems that I can see,___ the gleam-ing can-dle-light still shin-ing bright thru the syc-a-mores for me.___ The new mown hay___ sends all its fra-grance from the fields I used to roam. When I dream a-bout the moon-light on the Wa-bash, then I long for my In-di-an-a home.___

Johnson Rag

Ukulele tuning: gCEA

GUY HALL & HENRY KLEINKAUF

With a swing

Johnson Rag

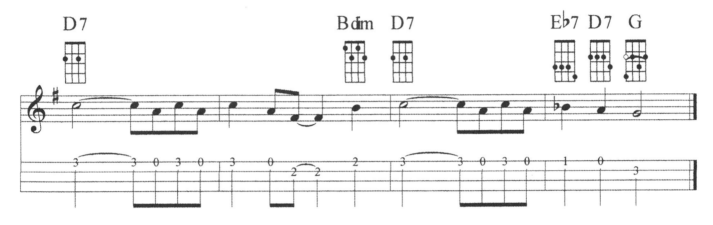

A classic version of the *"Johnson Rag" was recorded* by **Glenn Miller and his Orchestra** for RCA Victor in May of 1939.

Ma
(He's Making Eyes at Me)

Ukulele tuning: gCEA

SIDNEY CLARE

CON CONRAD

Ma (He's Making Eyes at Me)

Margie

Ukulele tuning: gCEA

BENNY DAVIS

CON CONRAD &
J. RUSSEL ROBINSON

Margie

F   D7

all   is   said   and   done,   there   is   real - ly   on - ly   one,   Oh!

Gm   C7   F

Mar - gie,   Mar - gie,   it's   you!

The song, *"Margie,"* was named after the 5-year old daughter of singer-songwriter, **Eddie Cantor.** Cantor, famous for his high-energy, bug-eyed performances on Broadway, radio, film and television made the song a chart-topping hit for 5 weeks in 1921.

Sylvester the Cat tortures **Elmer Fudd** with his late-night rendition of *"Moonlight Bay"* in the Warner Bros. / Merrie Melodies cartoon, *"Back Alley Oproar"* (1948).

"Moonlight Bay" was featured in the 1951 Warner Bros. film *"On Moonlight Bay"* starring **Doris Day** and **Gordon MacRae.**

The Beatles sang a lighthearted barbershop quartet-style version of *"Moonlight Bay"* on the *"Morecambe and Wise"* television show for the BBC in 1963.

Moonlight Bay

Ukulele tuning: gCEA

My Buddy

Ukulele tuning: gCEA

WALTER DONALDSON &GUS KAHN

My Buddy

Oh! You Beautiful Doll

Ukulele tuning: gCEA

A. SEYMOUR BROWN

MAT AYER

Oh! You Beautiful Doll

The legendary **Rosemary Clooney** recorded *"Oh, You Beautiful Doll"* for her solo debut with Columbia Records (Harmony) in 1949.

Peg O' My Heart

Ukulele tuning: gCEA

FRED FISHER

Peg O' My Heart

Bb

come, make your home____ in my   heart.____

School Days

Ukulele tuning: gCEA

WILL D. COBB

GUS EDWARDS

School Days

F7   B♭

I was your bash - ful bare - foot beau, and you

E♭6   Gdim7   B♭   D7   Gm

wrote on my slate, "I love you, Joe," when

C7   F7   B♭

we were a cou - ple of kids.

The infamous **Tiny Tim** (born Herbert Khaury), ukulele aficionado and musical archivist, was known for his eccentric persona and his trademark falsetto singing style. His repertoire contained many popular songs from the Tin Pan Alley era, and he was responsible for introducing these classic favorites to a new, young audience. He played *"School Days"* as well as several other songs on the *Ed Sullivan Show*, December 1st, 1968.

Second Hand Rose

Ukulele tuning: gCEA

GRANT CLARKE   JAMES F. HANLEY

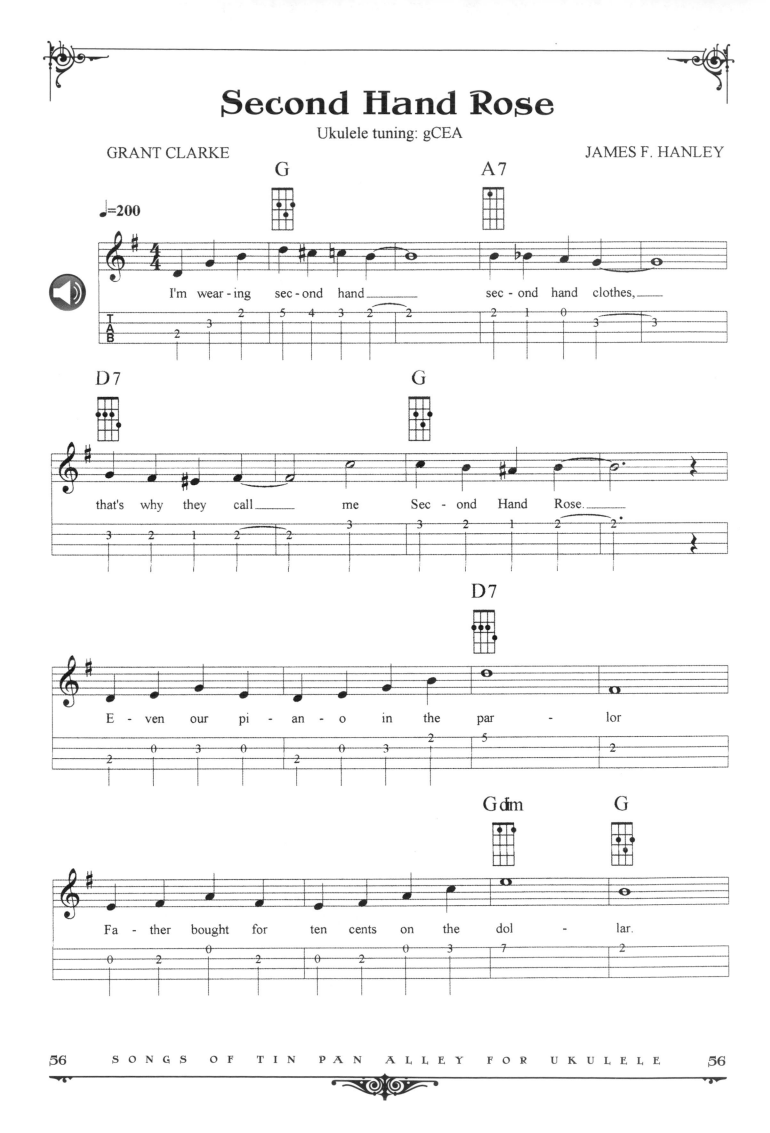

Second Hand Rose

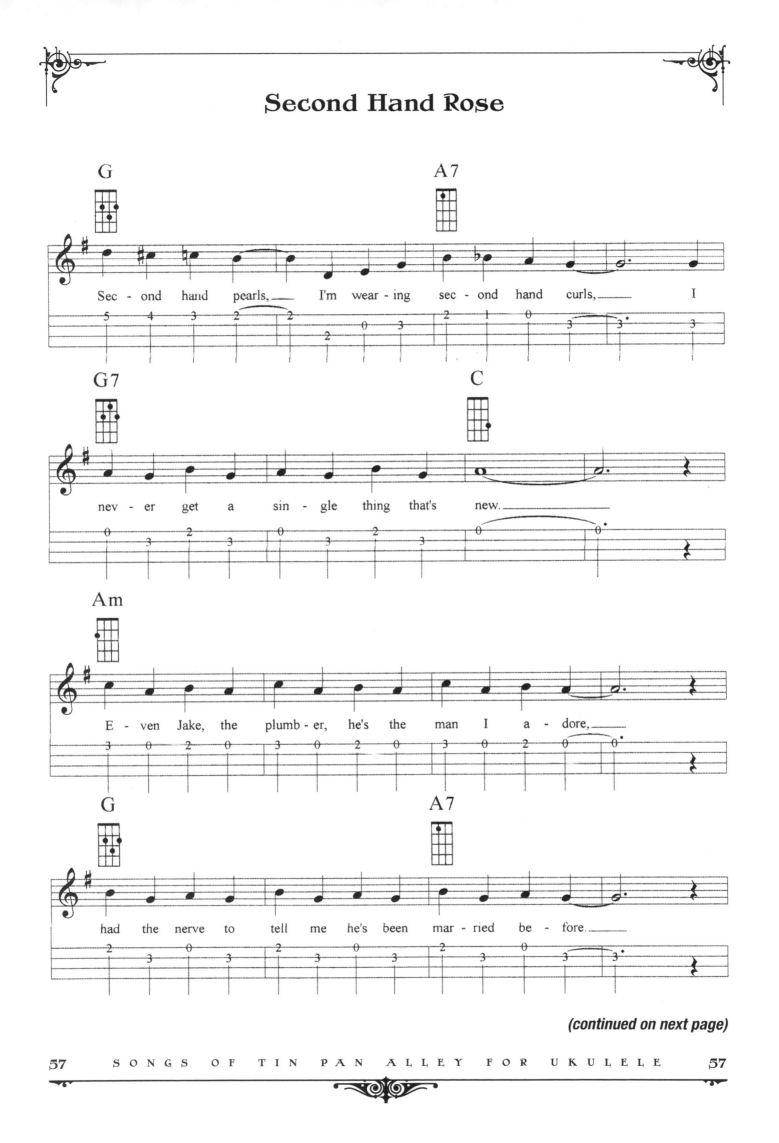

(continued on next page)

Second Hand Rose (continued)

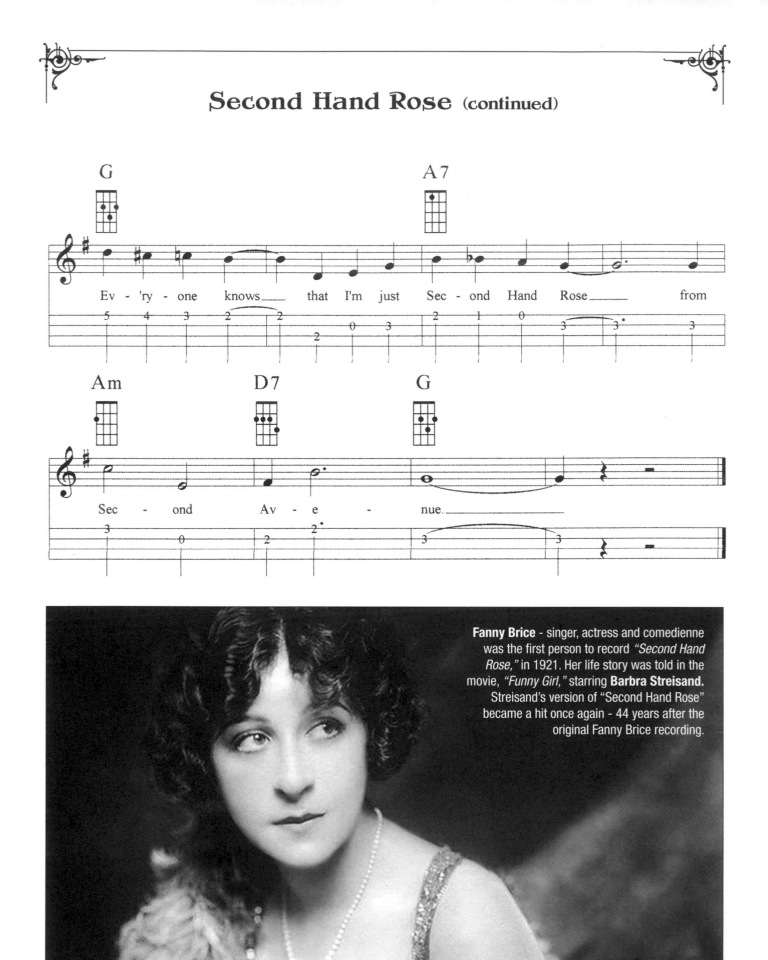

G   A7

Ev - 'ry - one knows____ that I'm just Sec - ond Hand Rose_____ from

5 4 3 2   2   0 3   2 1 0   3   3.   3
                           2

Am   D7   G

Sec - ond Av - e - nue._____

3   0   2   2.   3   3

Fanny Brice - singer, actress and comedienne was the first person to record *"Second Hand Rose,"* in 1921. Her life story was told in the movie, *"Funny Girl,"* starring **Barbra Streisand.** Streisand's version of "Second Hand Rose" became a hit once again - 44 years after the original Fanny Brice recording.

Shine On Harvest Moon

Ukulele tuning: gCEA

JACK NORWORTH

I Wish That I Could Shimmy Like My
Sister Kate

Ukulele tuning: gCEA

A.J. PIRON

I Wish That I Could Shimmy Like My Sister Kate

(continued on next page)

I Wish That I Could Shimmy Like My Sister Kate
(continued)

F7   Bb7   Eb 3fr.

shim - my   like   my   sis - ter   Kate.

The veritable "Queen of Shimmy" was **Marilyn Monroe** - seen here on the set of the classic comedy, *"Some Like it Hot"* (1959) in which she portrayed a ukulele player in an all-girl band. Sources are unclear as to whether or not she could actually play ukulele. She is posing here with a very rare white *Martin* uke.

Arthur Godfrey, radio and television icon of the 1950s was known for his love of the ukulele, which was featured in both his radio and television shows. His popularity caused a huge spike in the sales of ukuleles in the U.S.

Some of These Days

Ukulele tuning: gCEA

SHELTON BROOKS

Some of These Days

Take Me Out to the Ballgame

UKULELE TUNING: gCEA

JACK NORWORTH   ALBERT VON TILZER

George Herman "Babe" Ruth, Jr., known as the "Sultan of Swat" became a legendary baseball hero during the height of Tin Pan Alley. His career spanned an amazing 22 seasons, from 1914 through 1935.

There'll Be Some Changes Made

Ukulele tuning: gCEA

BILLY HIGGINS

W. BENTON OVERSTREET

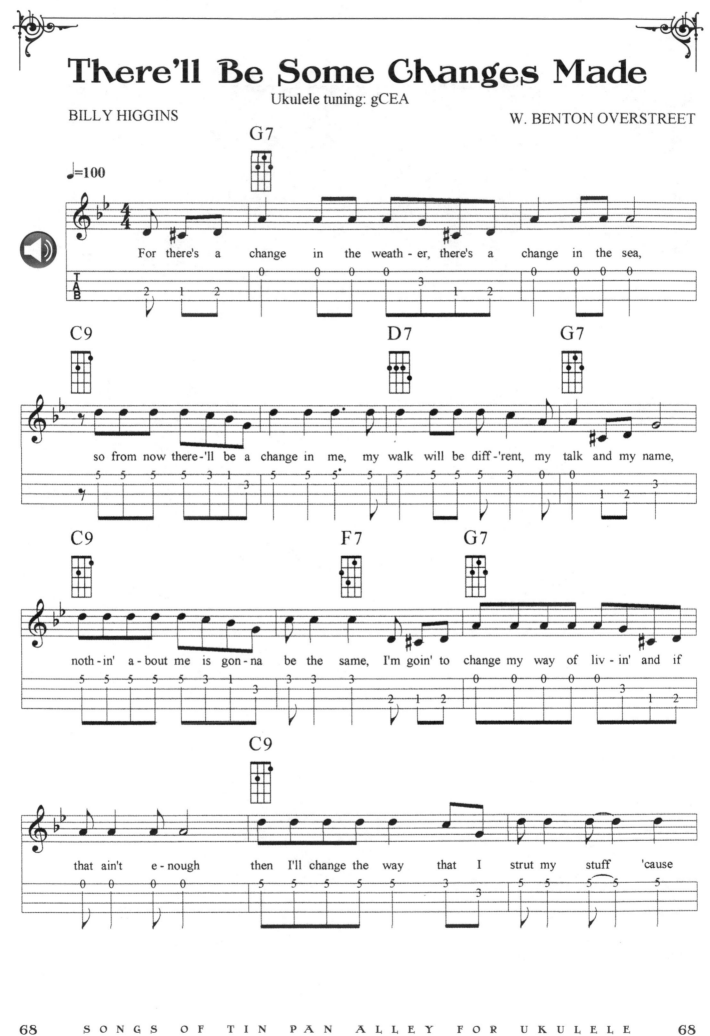

There'll Be Some Changes Made

Toot, Toot, Tootsie

Words & Music by
DAN RUSSO, GUS KAHN, ERNIE ERDMAN

Toot, Toot, Tootsie

(continued on next page)

Toot, Toot, Tootsie (continued)

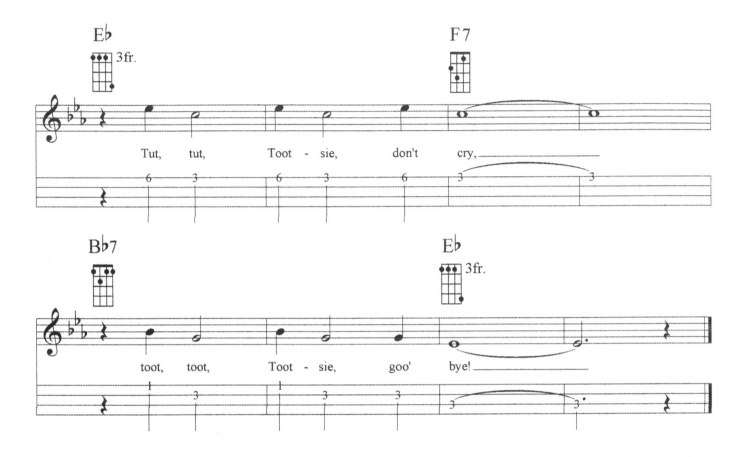

Eb   F7

Tut,   tut,   Toot - sie,   don't   cry,

Bb7   Eb

toot,   toot,   Toot - sie,   goo'   bye!

"Toot, Toot, Tootsie" was featured in the 1927 motion picture, *"The Jazz Singer,"* starring **Al Jolson** (pictured here with Eugenie Besserer). The movie is an important piece of cinematic history, in that it is the first feature-length film to include synchronized recorded dialogue sequences.

Twelfth Street Rag

Ukulele tuning: gCEA

Arranged by: DICK SHERIDAN

EUDAY L. BOWMAN

With an easy swing

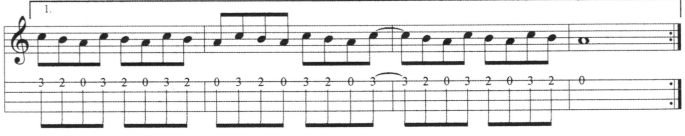

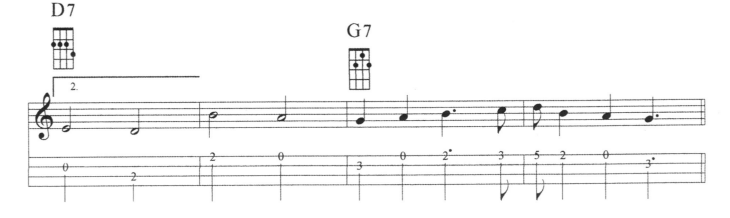

Twelfth Street Rag

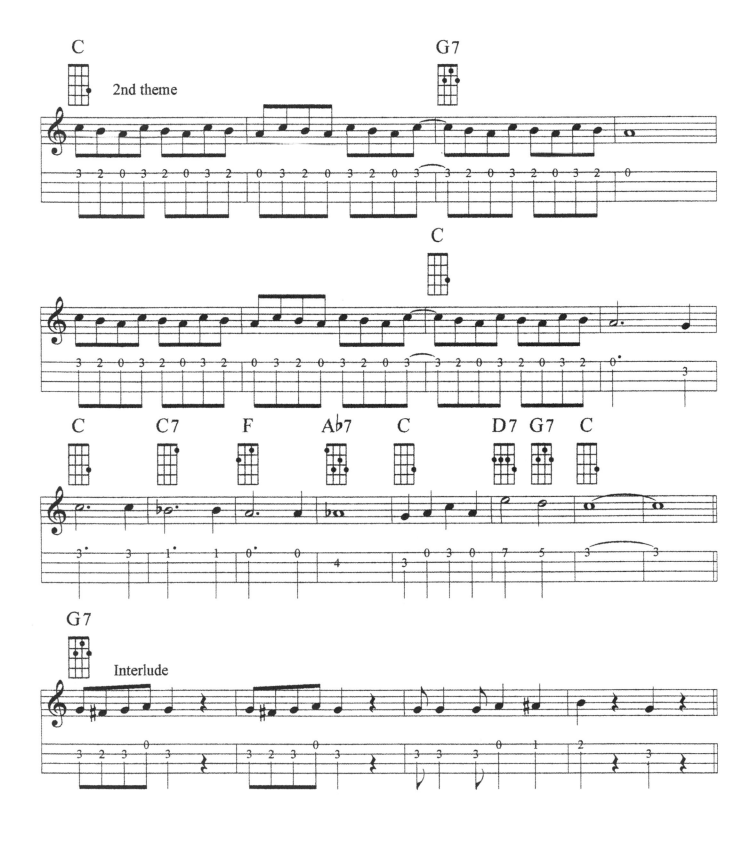

(continued on next page)

Twelfth Street Rag (continued)

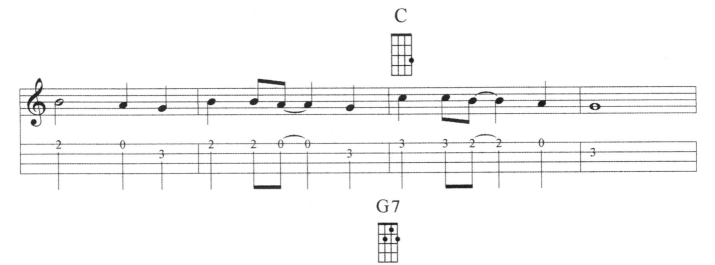

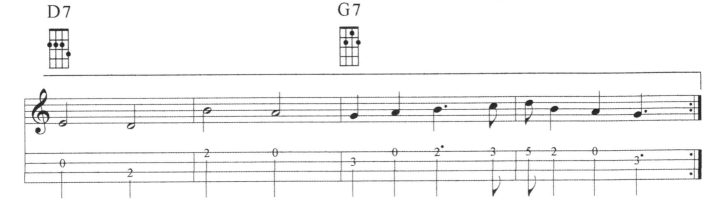

Twelfth Street Rag (continued)

Wait Till the Sun Shines, Nellie

Ukulele tuning: gCEA

ANDREW STERLING

HARRY VON TILZER

Wait till the sun shines, Nel - lie,

when the clouds go drift - ing by:

we will be ha - py, Nel - lie,

don't you sigh.

Wait Till the Sun Shines, Nellie

Whispering

Ukulele tuning: gCEA

JOHN SCHONBERGER

Whispering

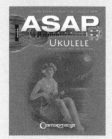

More Great Books from Dick Sheridan...